# The Lessons of the Earth

*Marc Maurer*
*Editor*

**Large Type Edition**

A KERNEL BOOK
published by
NATIONAL FEDERATION OF THE BLIND

ISBN 1-885218-28-1



Printed in the United States of America

# Table of Contents

The Lessons of the Earth
*by Marc Maurer* .......................................... 1

Take Me Out to the Ball Game
*by Eric Duffy* .......................................... 13

The Barbershop Pirate
*by Brian Miller* .......................................... 21

The Blessing of Braille
*by Adam Rushforth* .......................................... 39

Embracing Teenagers
*by Ruby Polk* .......................................... 45

Climb Every Hill
*by Sherry Ruth* .......................................... 50

Cherry Picking
*by Ramona Walhof* .......................................... 54

Falling Backwards
*by Doug Elliott*........................................ 66

Shooting Through the Screen Door
*by Nancy Scott*........................................ 75

# Editor's Introduction

It is early spring as this twenty-sixth volume in our Kernel Book Series is being prepared to go off to the press. Having grown up in Iowa where farming and gardening permeated both the culture and economy of the community in which I lived, my thoughts turn naturally at this time of year to images of planting, nurturing, and new growth.

I think of watching that which is planted sprout and, after struggling with the realities of weather, water, and weeds, spring forth into that which it was intended to be—often all the taller and stronger for having endured and conquered the uncertainties and challenges of the growing season.

I think also of the farmer and the gardener who are there through it all—early and late—loosening the hard soil, supplying it with nutrients, rooting up the weeds—hoping always for the plentiful harvest, knowing that such a harvest will be life-giving to the community.

These boyhood images are ever close to me even though I now live in a large city, and my hands rarely till the soil in the literal sense of my youth. But in another very real sense that is exactly what I, my colleagues in the National Federation of the Blind, and you who have joined with us through the Kernel Book Series are doing every day.

When we work to see that blind children and youth have the chance to learn Braille, we are preparing the soil. When a young blind boy learns all there is to know about baseball and devises a way for blind youngsters to share in the essentials of the game, the soil is enriched. When a mother finds a way to overcome her teenager's embarrassment about her blindness, the weeds are rooted up. When a talented blind

*Marc Maurer, President*
*National Federation of the Blind*

graduate student whose hobby is singing in a barbershop choir becomes the star of the show, the harvest is good, and the community is enriched.

And so I have named this new volume in our Kernel Book Series *The Lessons of the Earth*. For in it you will meet the people I just spoke of—whose lives, when intertwined with ours, truly reflect those lessons.

As we approach this new growing season we need those of you who have come to be our friends and coworkers through these pages more than ever. We need you to continue to believe in us, to see us as people you want to know and work with who have something to offer to the communities in which you live.

We need you to share what you have learned about us with others and to enlist them as co-tillers of the soil. For what you and we do now is of critical importance in the lives of blind children growing up today, in the lives of those in their mid years who become blind from accidents or eye diseases, and in the lives of the ever-increasing number of senior citizens who are experiencing serious vision loss through the effects of aging.

The garden we plant together today, and the nurture that we give it, will determine the coming harvest. We in the National Federation of the Blind have always found *The Lessons of the Earth* to be good. With your help, they will continue to be so.

Marc Maurer
Baltimore, Maryland
2004

# WHY LARGE TYPE?

The type size used in this book is 14-point for two important reasons: One, because typesetting of 14-point or larger complies with federal standards for the printing of materials for visually impaired readers, and we want to show you what type size is helpful for people with limited sight.

The second reason is that many of our friends and supporters have asked us to print our paperback books in 14-point type so they too can easily read them. Many people with limited sight do not use Braille. We hope that by printing this book in a larger type than customary, many more people will be able to benefit from it.

# The Lessons of the Earth

by Marc Maurer

My wife Patricia and I have been blind all of our lives, yet we became parents twenty years ago. These facts seem simple and straightforward, but they contain an element of drama because we have not always known deep within us that we had the fortitude and the skill to raise children.

David, who was born first, was subject to Sudden Infant Death Syndrome, and we worried about how to keep him alive and nourished. Dianna, who came later, had jaundice. She contracted many, many of the childhood ailments during her infancy. Because of her discomfort, she demanded much care.

Now, our children are almost grown. The problems they present to us are different from those of infancy, but they are just as troubling and just as demanding.

How do we teach them an appropriate approach to living? How much discipline should be imposed? How do we instill a spirit of independence while at the same time teaching our children of the dangers that exist? What is the proper balance, and how do we as parents get our teenagers to pay attention? The dangers of childhood are real, but the dangers of the teenage and young adult years are at least as real and sometimes more complex.

I grew up as a blind boy in the Midwest. My parents taught me what they thought I should know, but they had no experience with blindness, and they did not know what to expect.

Although there were variations in the ways my parents taught us, my mother usually insisted that we learn from books, but my father taught us to use our hands. We did not have what many children take for granted today—computers, VCR's, DVD players, cell phones, Game Boys, and other electronic devices. We did have a used television that my father bought for $50, but it gave out after a while.

When I was in high school, I bought a TV at an estate sale for $9.75. The picture on the television was no good, but I didn't care because I couldn't see it anyway. The sound worked well, and I listened to television programs for a number of months. When I learned that a local daycare center for underprivileged children had been robbed of its television, I had mine repaired and gave it to them. I thought the children might need it more than I did.

We played checkers, dominos, and cards; and we spent a lot of time outdoors. All of the kids in the Maurer household were expected to try to help with family chores and (if we could find a way to do it) with bringing in something else to support the family. We vacuumed the rugs, and scrubbed the bathroom, and washed the dishes, and took out the garbage.

Sometimes I was charged with the responsibility for hanging the clothes on the line to dry. While I was doing this one day, my mother told me that she never had enough clothespins to do the washing. I bought her some for her birthday. They cost me thirty-nine cents, which was quite a bit for me. Somehow the gift didn't go over very well.

One of my jobs was to help with the garden. My father had a prescribed plan for it. As soon as the days were warm enough, it was time to prepare the ground. My father told me that the earth of the garden must be turned with a shovel or a spading fork. He could dig with the shovel, but I didn't weigh enough to get the blade to pierce the ground. I preferred the spading fork. After the ground had been turned, it must be raked smooth. After the spading and raking, the plot of earth we used was black and rich—loose and smooth to the touch.

My father always did the planting himself. The rows of vegetables should be absolutely straight—he said. He put a stake in the ground at each end of the row and tied a string from one end to the other. Using the pointed edge of the hoe, he made about a three-inch trench along the line of the string, dropped in the seeds, and covered them with earth. With water to keep the ground moist, the plants began to sprout within a few days—radishes, bib lettuce, carrots, onions, corn, and many other vegetables.

My job was to weed the garden and to thin those vegetables that needed it. I learned to recognize the vegetable plants by touch. The sprouts that were growing side by side in a straight line with similar characteristics were certain to be the ones planted by my father. Those that were not in the proper place or that exhibited different characteristics were the weeds. These had to go. Some people cultivated their gardens with a hoe chopping the unwanted plants that had sprouted between the rows. However, I extracted the weeds by pulling them out one at a time.

Once my mother told me to weed the flower garden, but I got mixed up. Apparently the plants that I chose to weed were the ones that she had meant to keep. She sent me back to the vegetables.

Depending on the season, we picked blueberries and cherries or apples and pears. There was always some outdoor work to do around the house, and I was a part of it.

My father did home repairs, and he taught me. Replacing the washers in our faucets, installing window glass when panes had been broken, replacing the trim around a doorframe and similar jobs were a part of the weekend routine. I liked the tools, and my father let me help him. I gained an interest in mechanics, and soon became responsible for maintaining the lawnmower and repairing my tandem bicycle—a gift from my parents when I was about twelve years old.

I appreciated the teaching that my father gave to me, and I loved him dearly, but I often felt frustration with him. The world in which he lived seemed so very different from my own, and he sometimes challenged my assumptions without taking the time to explain why he thought they were wrong. As I think of my own children, I hope that I give them the reasons for the challenges I offer, but I sometimes fear that they feel as frustrated with me as I did with my own father.

When my son David was fifteen, he decided that he wanted a summer job. He did not want to spend the months away from school in idleness, and he did want extra spending money. I helped him find employment with a construction crew, and I arranged for transportation so that he could make it to the jobsite by 6:00 a.m.

At about the same time my daughter Dianna told her brother that she did not want to work. When he asked her about receiving spending money, she responded by saying, "Dad will give me whatever money I want."

However, when Dianna reached the age of fifteen she also decided to go to work. Today, she earns money serving as a cashier in a bakery. I have never worked in a bakery, but I have earned pocket money by baking bread for my neighbors when I was young. Dianna needs the money from the bakery because she persuaded her parents to buy her a Volkswagen convertible when she reached the age of sixteen, and she needs the money for gasoline.

She regards the convertible as hers, but her mom and I know it belongs to us. One complicating factor is that Dianna took the initiative to obtain the car. She decided what vehicle she wanted; she searched for it on the Internet; she identified the owner of the machine; she arranged for us to take the car for a test drive; and she stood by with a hopeful expression on her face while her dad negotiated the price. Without her active persuasion, we would not own the Volkswagen.

Blind parents who have sighted children find themselves in an anomalous position. Although Patricia and I own the Volkswagen, we are not able to drive it. Consequently, Dianna thinks of it as hers.

Dianna, who is now in high school, is planning to attend college, but she is worried about it. Will she be able to keep up with her studies? Will she like living away from home? Will she find ways to deal with the social pressures on the college campus? These and dozens of other questions pass through her mind.

We, Dianna's parents, wonder what we should do to help. We have observed that our daughter is a conscientious hardworking employee and that she does well in school. How can we help her find the courage she needs? I am confident she will do well, but I would like to show her that she need not feel such stress and tension in facing the decisions she must make.

In the spring when the earth warms and the days lengthen, I sometimes think about planting. However, I know that the first week of July is the time for the convention of the National Federation of the Blind, when more than 3,000 blind people will come together to talk about what plans we will make to bring greater opportunity for the blind of this generation and the next. Will blind children get Braille books? Will they have the chance to get a college education? Will they learn to ride bicycles and explore the great outdoors? Will they discover that they too can plant a garden?

These questions will be answered by the imagination and the planning at the convention of the National Federation of the Blind. Blind scientists and engineers, blind physical therapists and pharmacists, blind machinists and teachers along with those in hundreds of other professions will gather to decide what shall be done on behalf of the blind in the years ahead. Imagining the shape of tomorrow and planning to produce opportunity that does not yet exist are tremendously challenging. When the spring comes I think of these things and put my energy into them. But I miss the smell of warm earth and the crisp ripeness of fresh-picked homegrown vegetables, and I have a small regret that my children know less of these things than I have known.

Sometimes the harvest is from the earth. Sometimes the growth consists in advancing the public understanding of the needs and wants of the blind. Sometimes we measure the advances we make in our own capacity to believe in ourselves and to take combined action to build our own futures. In all of what we do, you have helped us by reflecting our belief in what we can do to contribute to the communities in which we live.

When I joined the National Federation of the Blind more than thirty years ago, I had not come to understand completely that I could grow plants or raise children or contribute to the development of our society. Working with my blind brothers and sisters and with you, I have gained this knowledge and the confidence to put it into effect. Working with you, I shall pass this knowledge to others who need it, and together we will plant our garden.

# Take Me Out to the Ball Game

by Eric Duffy

*Baseball is an American institution. It has meant many things to many people. It was as important to Eric Duffy growing up as a blind child as it was to his sighted brother. Today Eric is a leader in the National Federation of the Blind of Ohio. He has two young sons, and baseball is important to him in a different way. Here is how he tells his story:*

I am one of eight children, the only one with a disability in my family. My parents were devastated to learn that I was blind. They had no hope for any sort of a future for me, but as a child I never thought of myself as particularly different from sighted kids. I couldn't do some things very well, and I knew that, as we grew older, some of those things would be more significant. From an early age I knew that I would never be able to drive a car for example, so I always looked for things in common with my sighted siblings and friends. Sports was one of these.

True, I could not catch a football or hit a baseball the way others could, but I could learn everything possible about the games that I loved. There was a time when nothing was more important to me than baseball. I studied the game; I knew something about every major league team, something about every player, and everything about the Cincinnati Reds. Those great ball players of the early '70's—Johnny Bench, Pete Rose, Joe Morgan, Tony Perez, and many others—were my heroes. Cincinnati Reds broadcasters Marty Brennaman and Joe Nuxall brought the game to life for me as for thousands of others.

With their vivid descriptions of the game and my insatiable desire to learn all I could

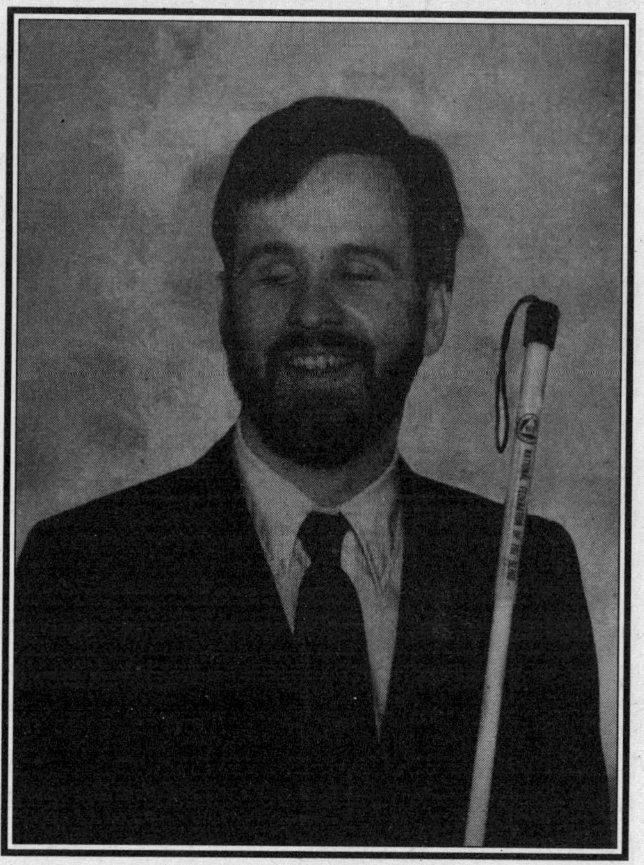

*Eric Duffy*

about the sport, I could hold a conversation about baseball with anyone—my parents, my brothers, or my parents' friends—it simply didn't matter.

I knew the game, and I could hold my own with anyone who wanted to talk baseball. I showed no mercy to anyone who challenged the vast superiority of the Big Red Machine to all other teams in the major leagues. No other catcher (living or dead) was in the same category as Johnny Bench.

At the time I was a student at the Ohio State School for the Blind, and although the doctors said I was totally blind, I had some usable vision through most of junior high school. Some of my friends had no vision at all, some just met the legal definition of blindness (20/200), and others were somewhere between the two. We wanted to find a way for all of us to play baseball together. We began by rolling a kick-ball on the ground. That way we did not have to worry about upper and lower strike zones.

We stipulated that the ball must be on the ground before reaching the plate. If it went over the plate without being hit, it was a strike. If it did not touch the plate and the batter didn't swing, it was a ball.

The standard rules of baseball applied—with the exception of having to roll the ball on the ground. Of course, as I have already said, we used a kick-ball rather than a baseball. First base was at the sliding board. Second base was a tree. Third base was a jungle gym. Home plate was a merry-go-round. Of course each of these objects had the appropriate base marker in front of it.

Someone at the base would clap or shout to guide a totally blind base runner. I was not fast, so I would hit the ball as far as I could, then slide headfirst into base because that's the way Pete Rose often did it. Some plays resulted in physical altercations. I remember talking about our games with my older brother, who was also playing informal games at school. We both expressed frustration at trying to get our teammates to understand that they could not run as fast as they could throw the ball. This is an important concept to understand when trying to put an opponent out. An accurately thrown ball reaches base long before the runner can.

At that time I did not know about the National Federation of the Blind, but it was then that I began to understand part of the NFB philosophy. I knew that, although my sighted brother and I were playing baseball under different conditions and different rules, the fundamentals of the game were the same. We enjoyed and loved the game in much the same way.

At home we used the same system, but the bases were orange cones. These were easy for me to see, and since my father worked construction, they were easy to get. As we got older, almost everyone got tired of this game. Those with enough vision to do so wanted to hit the baseball. The ball had to be in the air: no more rolling it on the ground. I, however, was determined not to be left out. I began pitching. I was taking a chance that the ball would hit me on a line drive, but it was a chance worth taking. I was still in the game.

The game of baseball has changed a great deal in the last thirty years. I don't enjoy it nearly as much as I once did. My own life is now very different as well. I now have two little boys, who are beginning to learn to play. I can throw the ball so they can work on their fielding skills. I can help teach them the fundamentals and history of the game. I go to practices and to games. I pay attention to the sound as the bat hits the ball, and I listen to the comments of people around me and on the field. When appropriate, I say, "Good hit, son." And at the end of the day, it never hurts to say, "Hustle a little more."

Whether we're talking about the game of baseball or the game of life, blind people can find ways to be successful. A very small percentage of the population earns a living in professional sports. So blind people aren't at much of a disadvantage with our lack of skills on the ball field.

As a blind person I know that, if I approach life in the same way that I approached baseball as a kid, I can be successful. But the key to success for blind people is good training and opportunity. Although good training can be hard to get, it is available. Equal opportunity is harder to win. More than 70 percent of working-age blind people are unemployed. Commitment to the dream of changing this prospect is one reason why I am a member of the National Federation of the Blind. In this as in many, many other ways we are changing what it means to be blind.

# The Barbershop Pirate

by Brian Miller

*Brian Miller lives in Iowa City, Iowa, with his wife Priscilla, who is also blind. Both are active members of the National Federation of the Blind, and both are two-time recipients of scholarships in the Federation's national scholarship program. Brian is working on a doctorate in history at the University of Iowa. In "The Barbershop Pirate" he demonstrates that success doesn't just happen. It has components: desire, hard work, persistence, belief, generosity—to name a few, and Brian puts them all to work in reaching his goal. Here is how he tells his story:*

What comes to mind when imagining a pirate? What do you see—a ship flying the Jolly Roger; men who haven't shaved or bathed in months with bandanas on their heads and cutlasses in their mouths? Does

*Brian Miller*

your imaginary pirate have a peg leg, a parrot, a bottle of rum, or perhaps a patch over one eye? How about a patch over both eyes? Can you imagine a blind pirate sailing the Caribbean in search of buried treasure and coastal towns to plunder?

Before joining the NFB I could neither imagine a blind pirate nor believe that I could play the part of a pirate on stage before hundreds of people. To me a pirate is more than an outlaw. A pirate embodies adventure, a willingness to take risks, to walk the plank if need be with the hope of making one's fortune. Growing up I always believed I had at least some of this pirate spirit in me.

When I became totally blind at the age of twenty-one, I thought my days of adventure might be over. In high school and college, one of the ways I exercised my pirate spirit was on stage, either acting in plays, or singing in choral ensembles. I had always been legally blind, but I did not use a white cane to get on or off the stage, or use Braille to learn my lines.

I feared that first moment of walking out on to the stage when the lights would hit my eyes and make me totally blind for several long minutes. I tried to fix this problem by peaking out from behind the curtains before I was to make my entrance, to get the shock of the lights out of the way before setting foot in front of the audience. Whatever I did, I was keen never to appear blind. After what little sight I had was lost, I could no longer use tricks to pretend I could see. I had either to learn new skills or hang up my cutlass for good.

A few years passed in which my personal pirate ship remained in dry-dock. I never lost my love of performing, however—especially my love of singing and music. I knew I had to find an outlet, some way to launch my pirate spirit, even if only to sail around the harbor. I never believed that my skills as a crooner would earn me a living—teaching would suffice to pay the bills—but I always knew I would have to make room for music somewhere in my daily routine.

A friend familiar with my love of singing suggested I check out the local barbershop chorus. This group sang all a cappella, and as an amateur group, provided an informal environment for men to turn their love of music into a hobby. I called the chorus secretary to find out when they had meetings, and he offered to pick me up and give me a ride. I thought this was terrific, since I did not drive, but I was nervous because I had not told this man I was blind.

He arrived at my door at 6:30 p.m. and whisked me off to chorus rehearsal without so much as a comment about my long white cane. At this time I was still unsure of myself as a blind person, often feeling acute embarrassment upon meeting strangers who did not know I was blind, fearing they might come unwound at discovering my blindness.

That first night of chorus I was pushed up onto the risers to sing with the whole group—some seventy-five men. A few guys moved over and made room for me in the tenor section. Some of them held sheets of music, which I could not see of course, but it did not matter.

Gary, the tenor section leader, leaned over to me and said, "Don't worry, half the guys here can't read music. Just listen to me and sing what I do." I did that, and I discovered quickly that my fellow chorus mates were far less interested in whether or not I could see, than whether or not I could sing. Some members of the chorus assumed that because I was blind, I was a natural virtuoso vocalist. I quickly proved that like many of my riser mates, I sorely needed ear and voice training before I would be singing at my full potential.

I was given learning tapes with my voice part on them so I could practice at home.

Many of the sighted chorus members used this same training technique.

That year I joined the San Diego Sunharbor chorus, and I also joined the National Federation of the Blind. My love of music had conquered my fear of going to places by myself where people did not know I was blind, but the NFB would give me the skills and confidence I needed to go much further. Confidence would mean not only asserting myself in situations so people unsure of my skills as a blind person would see quickly that I could do whatever I intended to accomplish, but confidence meant I would push myself further than I ever imagined I could go.

As a barbershop chorus member, I sang in annual shows, public exhibitions, and dozens of company holiday parties. As a tenor I was always in demand, and I was invited to sing with several quartets. Eventually I gained enough confidence in my own ability to begin my own quartet.

Several months after I joined the chorus, our group was getting ready to go to a barbershop regional competition. In the barbershop chorus and quartet world, competing is a major part of sharing the music and being an active member of the singing community. Choruses sing two songs before a large crowd and a panel of judges. In addition to singing, many choruses add some dance moves to their performance to catch the attention of the judges and to better sell the music as a package. Some six weeks before my chorus was to compete, the assistant director, a friend of mine, came up to me at the beginning of rehearsal and said, "The chorus music team was wondering what to do about you and competing."

Puzzled, I asked, "What do you mean, 'do with me?'"

"Well, we were not sure if you thought you would be able to learn the choreography for competition." I assured him I felt I was more than capable of doing the moves like the rest of the chorus, but even after hearing this he added, "Well, that's fine, but perhaps, if you don't mind, we might tell the judges ahead of time that we have a blind chorus member so they aren't caught, er, off guard." My friend was clearly uncomfortable, and I was unsure how to respond. I was fairly certain I could learn the moves adequately enough, but I also didn't want to risk costing my chorus points if somehow I wasn't in sync with the rest of the group while on stage.

How far should I push for my right to prove myself as a blind person? What if I insisted that they not tell the judges? Would they still let me perform? Was I ready to put my skills to the test when it could affect the whole group?

I considered all this for a moment, then offered, "Since there are still a few weeks before we compete, why not let me work on the choreography with everyone else between now and then, and then the music committee can decide whether or not to inform the judges about my blindness." The assistant director agreed to this, so I embarked on an intensive effort to learn all the choreography for the competition. I was determined that I would go on stage with my chorus mates without any judge being warned ahead of time that I was blind. It was not that I was embarrassed to be blind; I simply wanted to show that I could perform at the same level as everyone else on stage, and that no exceptions or excuses needed to be made because of my blindness.

The next week I went to chorus rehearsal early and found our chorus choreographer and said, "Bill, could you please show me exactly how to do the moves for these songs?" He agreed, and we met each week half an hour before rehearsal started to work together.

"The trick is," Bill told me, "to remember that each move is meant to emphasize the words of the song. So, once you figure out which move goes with which words, you always know when to move." He would describe the move to me, then show me by either letting me feel how his hands moved, or by moving my hands or arms to demonstrate exactly how each step was to be done.

"So," Bill would say, "when you hear this phrase, start moving your hands up to the side of your head, and make jazz hands."

"What are jazz hands?" I asked.

"Oh, hold your hands palm out to the audience and spread your fingers apart and then shake your hands back and forth like sparklers."

"Got it."

Numerous repetitions allowed me to internalize the choreography so I could sing and move at the same time, and not worry every minute about whether I had it exactly correct. Other chorus members could watch each other, or look in a mirror to gauge whether they had it right, but with practice, I could do the same moves without such references.

I heard nothing from the music team until the weekend of the competition. The assistant director came up to me to ask how I was feeling about my first competition with the chorus. I told him I was excited and couldn't wait for our chance to show our stuff.

He then turned to go, but came back to me as if something had just occurred to him. "Oh yeah, I wanted to tell you we decided that there won't be any need to tell the judges about you ahead of time. Also, we were wondering if you would mind moving to the front row, as we think you could add a lot to the chorus's look." The front row was where all the guys with the best smiles, the best singing faces, and the most confidence with the moves were placed. I told my friend of course I would be happy to move up to the front. I didn't tell him how much it meant to me that they had confidence in me and that I had proven to them that their concerns about my abilities were unnecessary.

When I left San Diego some five years ago and moved to Iowa, I knew I wanted to keep singing. I quickly found a barbershop chorus in my new town and joined its tenor section. This was a smaller, quieter chorus, and Midwesterners seemed more reserved and wary by my California standards.

I worried a little about what they would think of a blind guy joining their chorus, but more importantly, I wanted to do more now than just sing. I wanted to be a part of the music team and be involved in deciding what the group would sing and where we would perform. I wanted to show that I was not just a voice, but that I could be a leader. I needed more than acceptance on their part, but I needed to prove that I had skills to offer.

I had been teaching myself music theory, and learning Braille musical notation. I had attended music and vocal performance workshops, and chorus officer training seminars. I rarely missed a rehearsal, and I was on stage for every show and competition and community performance.

It took some time, a few years in fact, of quiet, persistent commitment to my new chorus, but it paid off. After singing with the Iowa City Old Capital Chorus for a couple of years, the chapter president approached me and asked if I would consider serving on the board as music VP, an elected position. My job would be to work with the director and assistant director to select all the music the chorus would sing and develop each week's rehearsal agenda, as well as the themes and music for our annual shows and competitions. I agreed to serve, and I was elected unanimously. Again, it is unlikely that my chorus mates fully appreciated what it meant to me as a blind person to be elected to the chorus board, but this was fine—they did not need to know.

It was more important to be serving my chorus and showing what I could do, than to be admired or told I am an inspiration and never be asked to contribute. Being an active member of my chorus is another way of being part of my community, as I stand on the risers with other teachers, mechanics, administrators, lawyers, and pharmacists.

There was one more step I wanted to take, to push myself further as a performer. I wanted a speaking role in our chorus's annual show. I had been afraid to audition for a speaking role as those with larger parts in our shows had to move about the stage and interact with other actors as well as the audience. After a couple of years of indecision, I finally mustered the courage and confidence to audition for a part. That year our show featured pirates who sang barbershop—something of a fantasy, obviously. I told the show manager I wanted to try out for a speaking part. He mentioned it to the scriptwriter, and he suggested I try playing the part of Seymour, nephew to Captain Black Angus.

I had the script sent to me via email, and then I downloaded it to my portable note taker which I took to script rehearsals. I read for the part, and everyone agreed I was a perfect Seymour, the pirate who wore two patches. I used a long sword instead of a white cane to get around the stage. I had to follow the captain on and off the pirate ship, and even out to the edge of the stage. We were pirates that sang and danced in the best Gilbert and Sullivan tradition.

I wanted to be sure that moving around the stage during the performance would not be a problem. I did not want to be the pirate that stumbled rather than plundered.

Hours before the show, I spent some time exploring the stage and familiarized myself with all the props and the layout of the fabricated pirate ship. I practiced moving about with my sword, which I used just as I would my white cane. The difference this time was that I knew I could do it—and do it well. I no longer feared my blindness would be "discovered," or that I would be a detriment to my chorus.

There were more than 800 in the audience, and our show was a big hit. My chorus mates never expressed any doubt that I could do it, but I know that after the show they had new reason to trust in my abilities.

My wife later recounted several conversations she overheard in the foyer. One woman said to another, "How did that one pirate see with those patches over his eyes?" And another woman who knew me responded, "He couldn't see, he was really blind." To which the first woman said, "But how did he get around the stage like that?"

The answer is that I used the same skills blind people use every day to get to work, to care for their families, or to participate in their favorite hobbies.

Without the NFB I would probably still have joined a chorus, but it was the confidence gained from my involvement with the NFB that pushed me to do more. As a blind person it is sometimes too easy simply to be a passenger, a passive participant. I wanted to be active, to be involved in the direction my chorus took, and to take charge of the hobby that was such an important part of my life.

Truthfully, wearing two patches was a bit uncomfortable, and everyone in my chorus called me Seymour for months after the show, but I don't regret for one second letting my pirate spirit loose on the world and taking up my sword which, at least for that night, was mightier than the pen.

# The Blessing of Braille

by Adam Rushforth

*Adam Rushforth is a student at the National Federation of the Blind's Louisiana Center for the Blind, where he is learning Braille. In his story he describes the exhilaration he felt when he was able to read a book on his own and give a talk in his church using Braille notes he wrote himself. Here is what he has to say:*

My whole life I have been a blind person who thought I could succeed in life living like a sighted person. I learned Braille when I was in the fourth and fifth grade but never used it to do any of my schoolwork. I thought it was exciting to learn how to read Braille, but never was willing to put in the time actually to become proficient in Braille. I remember my first convention in

Philadelphia with the National Federation of the Blind when I heard a talk on the television in the hotel from Kenneth Jernigan. In that talk, he mentioned a blind woman who had a three-year-old child come up and ask her to read her a story. What would I do if a future child of mine asked me to read to him or her, I thought. The image of pressing "play" on a recorder, or pressing the speak button on my computer did not appeal to me. It was at that time that I realized that I was on the verge of becoming illiterate. I never considered that even when I went totally blind I was illiterate. I still ponder this thought as I am struggling to read Braille.

From the third grade to the fifth grade my mother and father would read to me all of my assignments. They would sit with me until all hours of the night to help me complete my homework, which sometimes included reading entire novels. It was at this time that my mother insisted that I learn how to read Braille. During the fourth and

*Adam Rushforth*

fifth grades I learned to recognize the Braille code. At the end of my fifth-grade year I received a closed circuit television (CCTV), and this made me feel independent again. My mother still insisted that I learn Braille, but I used the Braille class to do my other class assignments. I struggled through school using magnifying glasses and the CCTV.

Recently, I have recognized that it is imperative that I receive proper training to improve my blindness skills. Learning Braille became a burning desire of mine. Before I entered the National Federation of the Blind's Louisiana Center for the Blind, I was timed reading Braille at 25 words per minute. I have now been at the center for just over four and a half months, and I have been timed at 78.2 words a minute. Even more exciting, for the first time in my life I have read a book in Braille. It is probably the first book that I have really read since the first grade. I had always had someone else read me the books, listened to books on tape, or had the computer read them to me. What a wonderful feeling it is to know that I am actually literate and can read a book on my own.

The bishop of my church asked me if I would give a talk at church the following week. I got on my computer and used the Internet to find scriptures and talks by church leaders on the topic that I was assigned. I studied and researched the subject and found some scriptures and stories that I wanted to use in my talk. Usually I would have spent hour upon hour memorizing the scriptures and the stories word for word. This time I decided to try something different. The night before I was to give the talk I Brailled out the scriptures and stories with my slate and stylus. It took me about an hour instead of the five or six it would have taken me if I had tried to memorize it all.

That night I read the things that I had slated about three times. The next morning I read them about two more times. I wanted to make sure that I could read those things that I had written at a speed that would be comprehensible. When I gave my talk, I said a lot of it in my own words. But when I wanted to share the things that I wanted to say verbatim, I read them from the paper that was in front of me. At that time I felt extremely grateful for the privilege that I had to be able to read Braille.

All of my life I desired to be able to read notes or share a story without having to memorize them. Giving the talk in church gave me a sense of empowerment, not that I take any glory from God, but I thank him for allowing me this blessing of learning Braille that I would use in my life. I now read the hymns and follow along in the scriptures during church, which is a blessing that until now has never been afforded me. I am filled with joy for such a blessing in my life.

# EMBRACING TEENAGERS

by Ruby Polk

*Ruby Polk is a member of the National Federation of the Blind of Missouri. Her children were teenagers at the time she became blind. Their adjustment to her blindness was perhaps as difficult as her own. Here is how she tells her story:*

When I first began to lose my sight from glaucoma, I experienced a great deal of difficulty with my teenagers.

The greatest challenge was to address the issue of embarrassment. My two teenagers, ages fourteen and sixteen, were quite popular in school and community activities. They had many friends coming and going in our home all the time. So when I began to lose my vision and was unable to do the things that I used to do, such as driving a car, taking dictation at Scout meetings, identifying colors, looking up numbers in the telephone book, and cooking barbecue on the grill, I started seeing a trend of their friends coming over to the house less and less.

I observed this declining situation for months. I finally decided to embrace my son and daughter and ask them to share their feelings with me. I asked them to be open and honest about my blindness.

The first thing they said was that their friends felt very uncomfortable coming over to the house because of my blindness. They were embarrassed when people looked at me in a pitiful way. They wanted me to be able to see again and do the things that I used to do. They thought they had lost their mother.

At that moment, I realized that this was my fault. I had not taken the initiative and

*Ruby Polk*

time to become a competent blind person. I explained to Lilly and Damon that I would never be able to see again. However, I offered them a proposal. I informed them that I would enter a structured rehabilitation center and get blindness training so that I could return to doing many of the things that I used to do, if they would go back to doing the things that they used to do with their friends.

My teens and I agreed to work together to accomplish this important goal. Also, in return, they said that they would encourage their friends to come over to our home and resume the fun activities as before.

I entered a rehabilitation center in California and learned Braille, orientation and mobility, daily living skills, CPR training, and social and interactive skills from competent blind instructors.

After returning home, my teenagers anxiously observed my independence in performing many tasks and embraced me. They eagerly waited to see how I used the blindness skills that I had learned. I became a big hit with them, and they even insisted that I go to the mall with them to select clothing. Also, they asked me if I wanted to accompany them to other places such as the amusement park so I could drive bumper cars if I chose to do so.

Openly embracing my teenagers about my blindness was the best thing that I could have ever done. I also became a much happier, productive person. Damon and Lilly are now young adults with children of their own. Explaining blindness to their children is much easier since they were exposed to blindness as teenagers in a positive way.

# Climb Every Hill

by Sherry Ruth

*Sherry Ruth is an active member of the National Federation of the Blind of Ohio. She serves as treasurer of the state organization and president of the Lorain County chapter. Here she relates an incident that helped reinforce her personal confidence. Here is what she has to say:*

When my son Tony was nine years old, we agreed to let him go away to church camp for a week. Brenda, the mother of Tony's friend, and I accompanied them to camp. When we asked where our sons would be staying, someone pointed to a cabin at the top of a very high hill. I was skeptical about making the climb over such rough terrain, because I had been blind for several years

*Sherry Ruth*

and was not sure that the climb was possible for me.

Luckily, I had recently joined the National Federation of the Blind and had learned that just about anything is possible if you have courage and confidence in yourself. My friend Brenda told me that the hill was full of pieces of wood sticking out of the ground, and weeds and rocks covered the area as well.

I could have stayed down below and let her take my son to his cabin, but I felt it was my job as his mother and decided not to let a little thing like blindness stop me. I have to say it was very difficult, and a few times I almost lost my footing—but I was determined.

When I reached the top, Tony's camp counselor was standing there. After I let out a big sigh of relief, I told him that I thought the climb up was rather dangerous. He cockily told me that I should try it in the dark if I wanted to know what tough was. With great pride I was able to tell him that I just had.

The remarkable thing was that my girlfriend had not noticed that several yards away was a sturdy wooden stairway. Needless to say, we took the easy way down. I am glad we did not know there was an easier way, because sometimes you need to challenge your ability as a blind person to take risks to realize you are a strong and competent member of society. The National Federation of the Blind has taught me not to be afraid to climb every hill.

# Cherry Picking

by Ramona Walhof

*Ramona Walhof grew up in a small town in Iowa. She has been an active leader in the National Federation of the Blind for nearly forty years. She now lives in Boise, Idaho, where she operates her own business and enjoys her home and grandchildren. Kernel Book readers have enjoyed her many previous insightful stories. Her current offering, "Cherry Picking," continues her presentation of blindness as just one of the many factors in a full and rich life. Here is what she has to say:*

When I was a child and attended the school for the blind, one of the things that happened the first day or so after we returned home for the summer was that my mother would take us all to the garden. We lived in a small house with almost no yard, so my mother would rent an area somewhere else in town for a garden. She wanted the vegetables she could raise, but she also liked to garden. Often by the time my brother, sister, and I came home from school, some vegetables would already be producing something to eat. The carrots and radishes would be first. But there would also be vegetables that were not yet planted. Sometimes we would plant cucumbers and melons. The musk melons (native to Muscatine, Iowa) would almost never be ready before we had to go back to school in late August or September, but the cucumbers would be ready to pick and make pickles while we were still at home.

I can remember planting corn at least once, although I think it was often planted before we got home. And some years we didn't grow corn. It took up a lot of space, and we had friends and relatives who lived on farms and grew a lot of Iowa corn.

The best part of gardening for me (and I suspect for many people) was picking and eating the vegetables. My grandmother made lots of pickled beets. My brother and sister and I loved pickled beets and talked our mother into growing enough beets that we could also make some into pickles. We had leaf lettuce, which we would eat with sugar and cream just as often as with salad dressing. We had peas and beans. I can remember shelling peas and snapping beans on our front porch.

Whether we raised it or not, we always had corn during July and August. Although many people find it hard to believe, there is nothing quite like field ripened Iowa sweet corn. It is wonderful to eat right off the cob. Most people spread butter all over it and use salt and pepper, too. Gradually, I learned that the best way for me was just plain, crunchy sweet corn.

My sister and I were soon recruited to help cut the corn off the cobs so that we could freeze it. We rented a locker in town where we would keep meat and frozen vegetables. Corn was kept in the locker after it was prepared in pint or pint-and-a-half boxes. No one complained if we would pop bits of corn into our mouths as we worked cutting it off the cobs. Sometimes ten or twelve kernels or more would stick together in a group, and they were very good to eat, partly cooked and ready to freeze.

Blindness was never much of an issue that we were aware of. Perhaps we were not required to do as much weeding and hoeing as we would have done if we had had good vision. However, we did some. We were told that weeds had different leaves from the vegetables, and they tended to grow between rows, while the vegetables did not. Carrot and onion tops were like threads or strings. Some weeds grew faster than the vegetables, too.

When picking tomatoes we were directed by our mother to the ones that were the most red. We were to leave the green ones so they could continue to ripen on the vines, although, we knew that a few green tomatoes could sit in the windowsill and continue to ripen.

We canned tomatoes whole, and we made juice. Sometimes we made apple butter and applesauce. But we did not have fruit trees. We canned green beans in quart jars, and we made bread and butter pickles. We never had enough carrots or peas to can. If we did not raise something we wanted to can, we often got fruit from relatives or bought it by the bushel. I never thought much about having a garden. It was just something we did in the summertime.

After I was married, my husband and I bought a house with a huge yard. I had no desire to plant a garden, and we did not want to spend the money to buy all the garden tools we would have needed. However, there was a huge grape arbor already well established in our yard. My husband said he liked grape juice. He was diabetic, so grape jelly was not much in demand. I called my mother and learned that grape juice was not much different to make from grape jelly. While my husband was alive I made about forty quarts of grape juice a year—grape juice with no sugar added. My husband said it was not quite as sweet as Welch's, but that was good, and there never was any left.

When my children were little and I was a single mother working full-time, I had no garden and did very little canning or freezing. Then when I bought a house in Boise in the early nineties, it had a big yard, much bigger than I wanted. My kids were grown up and away from home, and I was not looking for yard work to do. I was beginning to travel a lot for the National Federation of the Blind and for my work, another good reason not to have a big yard. But I liked the house and its location, and the yard would not go away.

In Boise you have to irrigate to keep grass alive. Watering is easy. You just have to move the sprinklers around to cover all the grass and shrubs. When I am away from home, it just has to wait unless I manage to arrange for someone else to stop by and water. Some people have automatic sprinkling systems, and some day perhaps I will.

After I bought this house, a young friend of mine with a small child and no yard said she would like to grow a garden and let her child play in the yard while she worked there. I was agreeable. Again it was fun to have a few home-gown vegetables. There was something in the yard that no one could recognize. After we began to water them, we found that they were two small peach trees, and by and by they bore peaches. I love peaches, so I decided to take care of them.

Dark sweet cherries grow very well in southwest Idaho, so I put in two small cherry trees. They were supposed to be dwarfs, but they are now quite large. And by and by they began to bear cherries. There were also lots of grapes, some at each end of the yard.

Way too soon my young friend moved many states away, and I gave up gardening.

I am still not a gardener, and I do not always manage to arrange for the trees and grapes to get thinned when they should. Sometimes they get fertilized, but not always. We do cut the grapes out of the cherry trees when they decide to attach themselves. Some years I have contracted with professionals to work in my yard, and I have a neighbor who wants the job, so I have never become a gardener. Recently, I replaced some roses I inherited from the previous owner with nice sod. The roses smelled good, and people liked them, but I didn't take very good care of them, and I like the grass better.

The cherries and peaches are fun! I have to compete with the magpies for the cherries. I can't let them get as ripe as I would like or the magpies will eat them all! But I don't mind eating them a little bit tart. And they will continue to ripen inside the house for a couple of days as well. This year I have been picking cherries for a week and taking them to work and giving them to friends.

Today I am on my way to Seattle where my daughter and her husband live. Tomorrow is a baby shower for their first baby, and of course I have to go. I am taking along a bag of cherries off my tree. I picked them this morning at about 7:00, so they are nice and fresh. When I get back in a couple of days, there will not be any left on that tree, because the birds will have had them. But this year the two trees are not on the same schedule, and I am hoping to have a few more from the other tree. It does not have as many cherries as usual, but it has some. Cherries are one of the pleasures of the summer for me; peaches come in September. The birds let me have most of the peaches, and I let them have the grapes.

My next challenge in the yard is to get rid of the gopher that has come in uninvited. He is not welcome, so we will try to scare him off with red pepper first; a trap if the pepper doesn't work; and poison if we must. In July I will have some picnics in the back yard where there is an above-ground pool and a good spread of grass.

If I could see, I would read more about plants, tools, chemicals, etc., that are available for use in yards. However, I rarely think about it. Occasionally, I inquire in stores, but the big discount ones do not provide as much information to their help as the little neighborhood stores used to do. Sometimes I have a reader look up something in a magazine or catalog, but mostly I don't use my reader time that way. Automatic scanners are wonderful, but they do not work well where there are a lot of pictures and headlines. That takes care of most catalogs and gardening magazines. Gardening still isn't a high priority for me. Mostly, I guess and compare notes with someone else in the neighborhood.

In the National Federation of the Blind, I have learned that I can do lots of things that many sighted people feel reluctant about expecting blind people to do. However, I have also learned it is okay not to try to do everything just to prove a blind person is able to do it. I have no desire to be a super blind person. I do wish to carry my share of responsibility in whatever group I happen to find myself. Occasionally, the part of the work I do may be determined partly by the fact that one of my characteristics is that I cannot see. However, at least as often the part of the work I do will be based on interest and experience.

I have no desire to drive my son's boat, but I am looking forward to trying out the water-skis some weekend this summer. Tomorrow I am scheduled to go kayaking with my daughter and her husband. I have never been kayaking before, and will do as I am told.

When it comes to my yard, I have to be in charge, but I will recruit help for many specific tasks. I like to do a little entertaining outside, and I thoroughly enjoy relaxing and working out in the pool. But in a good year, the cherries and peaches are the highlights of the summer at my house. Picking and eating them are still the best part of gardening.

# Falling Backwards

by Doug Elliott

*The National Federation of the Blind is made up of many individuals who work together to change what it means to be blind for themselves and for others. Doug Elliott is one of these individuals. How he came to be an active leader in the Federation is the subject of his story, "Falling Backwards." Here is what he has to say:*

I had never thought much about personally being a member of a minority group. I think I have as much social conscience as any other American, but minority-group status isn't something I had experienced myself. It was something I thought about as affecting other people and studied in college and graduate school while earning degrees for my profession as a social worker. Then, suddenly, I kind of fell backwards into thinking in a very personal way about how minority groups think and feel and function as a part of the larger American society. It happened to me like this:

A friend and I, both of us living in the state of Nevada, received an invitation to visit a national center providing services to a particular minority group. As I closed the door of the bedroom I was staying in at the center, I heard over the p.a. system a strong, resonant voice offering the opportunity for people in the building to sample strawberries and order cases of that tasty treat if they wished to do so.

I had heard this same voice many times before on recordings, during which this national leader explained to the minority group he served how it was possible to live as an equal to their peers in the world. This time he was selling strawberries. Some people called him Dr. J. Others called him Dr. Jernigan. What I heard was the voice of a leader talking to colleagues about the ordinary everyday pursuits everyone shares, like finding good stuff to eat and letting others in on the good fortune of a discovery.

Then I heard a second man's voice over the public address system. The man who owned this second voice had made some of the same kinds of speeches as Dr. Jernigan. The second voice was paging someone to call him at his office, a routine occurrence in offices all over the country—two colleagues getting together to get some work done. I had admired both of these men for months but had never met them in person. And here they were, so close and doing such ordinary everyday things.

Later that day, I met with Dr. Jernigan in his office, and we talked about helping members of the minority group living in Nevada to learn more about how they could gain independence and a greater role in the broader American culture. I told him I would try to help. He told me others had said the same thing but had then fallen short because the work was not easy.

That evening, we were both invited to dinner at Dr. Jernigan's home. He took us on a tour of his large and beautiful home, showing us areas of the home he had caused to be remodeled according to plans he designed himself and other areas he had remodeled, doing the work himself.

The food was wonderful, and the conversation ranged widely, always interesting. He was a grand host as was his wife. The evening was an ordinary dinner in the home of gracious people, made unusual by such good food and better company. I left feeling I would commit to helping the movement on behalf of this minority group.

The next morning my friend and I went to the house of the second man for breakfast. He was the elected president of the movement, as these men described the organization working on behalf of the minority group. I met the president's wife and two children. The president talked to us about current problems facing the organization in its mission to help minority group members and talked to us about how we could help. While he talked, he cooked breakfast for us. We ate with the family, then discussed more things happening in the movement before we left for the airport to go home.

One thing that had the current administration stirred up was that a national officer of the movement had been arrested and carried off an airplane for wanting to sit in the smoking section at the back of the plane and not in the front row where the airline had wished her to sit. The airlines thought they had the right to tell members of this minority group to sit anywhere they said and be taken care of by the airline staff.

The Second Vice president of the organization, Peggy Pinder, resisted this arbitrary treatment and was arrested for no logical reason and simply for not doing what she was told. I did not know Peggy but had a great deal of respect for the articles she wrote for the movement's magazine.

As we left for the airport, the president was preparing a grill for cooking meat later in the day. We thanked him and said we would help him where we could.

This all took place in 1987. It was my first meeting with the officers of the National Federation of the Blind: Dr. Jernigan, a school teacher, a director of services to the blind, and a longtime president of the National Federation of the Blind; and President Marc Maurer, a longtime leader in the Federation, a lawyer, and a husband with small children.

All the people in my story are blind except for Mrs. Jernigan. They all were doing ordinary things that sighted people do as we talked about the problems of the blind, and all of them live ordinary lives as blind people. Peggy is an attorney, city council member, and an involved politician in Iowa.

I learned that day that the ordinary everyday task can be completed as long as the blind person has the blindness training and confidence offered to all blind people by the National Federation of the Blind. These people all set an example for me, and I have tried to do the same thing since my first meeting with these leaders. Oh Yes, I am blind and currently living in Iowa with Peggy Pinder who is now Peggy Elliott.

I had been blind for twenty years when I visited the National Center. But I had never thought of myself as a member of a minority group.

Of course I knew I was blind and that I was working and raising a family. But I struggled daily with how I felt about myself and how others felt about me as a blind person. It didn't occur to me until I met these men with their strong voices and strong belief in me, a man they had never met, that I shared something with all blind people. These men taught me a precious lesson by the way they handled themselves; by the way they walked confidently through their everyday tasks; by the way they talked of great issues and shared a great find of strawberries; by the way they used their voices for advocacy on behalf of all blind people or to handle a simple task with a colleague; by the way they cooked and fed me while talking about helping others; by the way they reacted to a colleague's being arrested for standing up for her rights, believing they were personally involved even though they were not there—they taught me through the little things that they had a self-confidence born of their understanding of blindness I admired and wanted to acquire.

It was not the great sweeping words but the individual person-to-person kindness and casual competence that helped me to understand the simple fact that I am a member of that same minority group they belonged to and which they were encouraging me to join and help. The first step turned out to be understanding that I am part of that minority group!

For twenty years, I had stood apart from membership in the minority group. I was blind, but I felt I had nothing in common with other blind people. Then, simple acts of kindness by men who were themselves admirable opened the door for me to join and, more importantly, to want to join with them in the movement they led to take minority status and use it to forge a common bond through which positive change can be achieved. Now I understand I am a part of that minority group, the blind, and understand that I want to offer the same understanding to others, both to fellow blind persons and to the sighted persons among whom we live.

Join us and learn how to overcome stereotypes of blindness.

# Shooting Through the Screen Door

by Nancy Scott

*Nancy Scott lives in Easton, Pennsylvania. She enjoys writing, and her poems, stories, and articles have appeared in a wide variety of publications. Nancy credits her participation in the National Federation of the Blind's Writers Division with helping her to become a better writer.*

*How do young children form concepts about the world around them? Specifically, how does a young blind child learn the difference between "solid" and "not solid?" Nancy did it in a most interesting way. Here is how she tells her story:*

Playing with squirt guns is more fun when no one else is around. I'm not very good at shooting other kids with water. I guess this is because I can't see. Or maybe it's because other kids can see me aiming and move real fast and real quietly. But the water always goes where I want when I pretend, or almost always....

I'm on my back steps, squirt gun ready. I hear the hiss of Mom's iron in the pantry. I could shoot her, but not really. There's a door for the water to hit, so I can shoot her in my head.

I fire. The water sisses with the force of my wishing. Buzz against the screen so I know it's going where I want. Siss. Buzz. Pull the trigger. Feel the water going from the gun. Siss. Buzz.

"Stop that." Mom's voice.

That's not supposed to happen. Mom must be hearing me think. I know she does that sometimes.

"There's water all over the floor."

*Nancy Scott*

No. There's a door there. I'm six, and I'm not stupid.

"You're shooting through the screen."

That can't be, and I tell her. Water is big. It can stay in one place, not like air and noise. Air and noise are little, so they can go through the screen.

Mom sighs from mad to show-and-tell. "Wait," she says. I do, because I think she's still mad, and I know I'm right. "I have to turn off the iron."

Footsteps going and stopping and coming back. She puts my left hand inside the screen door, my right with the gun out and says, "Shoot."

Pull. Siss. Buzz. Wet. Wet against my inside hand.

"Come look." She opens the door farther and puts my right hand in the puddle on the floor.

I could have shot her after all.

And I think about trying to do just that to see if my ears could aim at the iron. But the screen doesn't feel like it has big enough holes in it. How far would the water go after it went through the screen? I don't ask out loud.

But Mom hears me think again. "No more shooting water through screens. If you do it again, no more squirt gun."

Was she still mad? And how could I be wrong about all this?

Next time it rains, I'll stand by a window with my hands on the screen to see if water really goes through it. After all, maybe Mom could trick me or maybe I am right sometimes. Maybe there has to be something pushing the water like wind.

But for now, I decide to remember that some water could go through screens and to practice my bad aim on the tree in the back yard. Mom has walked me around and shown me everything in the back yard. I can run all around it now and almost never hit even the clothes poles.

I'm allowed to go all the way down to the alley steps but not into the alley because cars can go there. Mom says that, soon, I will get a white cane, and I will learn to go farther with it.

Maybe I'll ask Dad later about how far water shoots through the screen. As long as Mom doesn't hear me ask, I bet he'll tell me.

# Other Kernel Books

*What Color Is the Sun?*

*The Freedom Bell*

*As The Twig Is Bent*

*Making Hay*

*The Journey*

*Standing on One Foot*

*When the Blizzard Blows*

*Toothpaste and Railroad Tracks*

*Tapping the Charcoal*

*Old Dogs and New Tricks*

*Beginnings and Blueprints*

*Like Cats and Dogs*

*Wall-to-Wall Thanksgiving*

*Gray Pancakes and Gold Horses*

*To Touch the Untouchable Dream*

*Remember to Feed the Kittens*

*Reflecting the Flame*

*Oh, Wow!*

*I Can Feel Blue on Monday*

*Reaching for the Top in the Land Down Under*

*Safari*

*Summit*

*Not Much of a Muchness*

*The Car, the Sled, and the Butch Wax*

*To Reach for the Stars*

# You can help us spread the word...

...about our *Braille Readers Are Leaders* contest for blind schoolchildren, a project which encourages blind children to achieve literacy through Braille.

...about our scholarships for deserving blind college students.

...about NFB-NEWSLINE®, a free service that allows blind persons to read the newspaper over the telephone.

...about where to turn for accurate information about blindness and the abilities of the blind.

Most importantly, you can help us by sharing what you've learned about blindness in these pages with your family and friends. If you know anyone who needs assistance with the problems of blindness, please write:

**Marc Maurer, President**
**National Federation of the Blind**
**1800 Johnson Street, Suite 300**
**Baltimore, Maryland 21230-4998**

# Other Ways You Can Help the National Federation of the Blind

Write to us for tax-saving information on bequests and planned giving programs.

OR

Include the following language in your will:

*"I give, devise, and bequeath unto National Federation of the Blind, 1800 Johnson Street, Suite 300, Baltimore, Maryland 21230, a District of Columbia nonprofit corporation, the sum of $__________ (or "____ percent of my net estate" or "The following stocks and bonds:_______") to be used for its worthy purposes on behalf of blind persons."*

## Your Contributions Are Tax-deductible